WESTERN

70 Years of Se

Stewart J Brown

Above: The Leyland Titan PD3 with
67-seat lowbridge body was one of
Western's favoured models from 1957
to 1961. An unusual choice of
bodywork for the Titans delivered in
1960 was Blackpool-based
Burlingham. There were 23 buses in
the batch, and the bodies were of a
design generally similar to that
produced by Northern Counties, as
seen on the 1959 bus on the left. *SJB*

Contents

A line of buses at Whitesands in 1959 starts with three buses belonging to Clarkes', and then over a dozen Western vehicles. Nearest the camera is a 1939 Leyland Cheetah with Alexander body, which Clarkes' operated from 1958 to 1960. It had been new to Alexander, and is standing alongside a Plaxton-bodied Foden, one of three bought new by Clarkes' in 1947-48. The double-decker, an ex Tynemouth & District AEC Regent, is still in its original owner's colours. The dozen or so Western vehicles include Bristols, Leylands, Guys and AECs. A bucket and mop leaning against the front of the Clarkes' Foden indicate some cleaning was in progress. *John Aldridge*

Acknowledgments

Many thanks to those photographers who kindly made material available for use in this book. Their work is credited individually. And a particular thanks to Gordon Bain and Garry Ward, who kindly read through a draft of the text and provided much additional information. For those who wish to keep abreast of developments the Western Enthusiasts Club publishes a bi-monthly journal. Details can be obtained from Gordon Bain at 12 Brisbane Street, Greenock PA16 8LN. *SJB*

First published 2002
ISBN 0-946265-35-8
© Bus Enthusiast Publishing Company, 2002
Typeset in Times and Helvetica
Electronic page makeup by Jeremy Scott

Published by
Bus Enthusiast Publishing Company
5 Hallcroft Close, Ratho, Newbridge
Midlothian EH28 8SD
Tel/Fax: 0131 333 2796
Email: enquiries@busenthusiast.com
Bus Enthusiast is an imprint of
Arthur Southern Ltd.

Foreword

WESTERN SMT, the direct predecessor of Stagecoach Western buses, came into being in 1932 but the company's roots can be traced back to the early days of motorbus operation in Scotland around the time of the first World War.

Today the company serves the south-west of Scotland, along with Arran, Bute and parts of Argyll, with a fleet of 480 modern buses and coaches. However in the past its operating area embraced Paisley and Greenock too, and the company operated the prestigious Glasgow to London service with some of the most luxurious coaches to be found anywhere in Britain.

The company's story is one of rapid growth in the 1930s and 1940s, followed by gradual decline from the 1950s as, like bus companies throughout Britain, it lost passengers as more and more people bought their own cars. The rise of TV ownership also hit bus use, as people stayed at home rather than going out to the cinema. But the company has experienced a remarkable renaissance during the 1990s, as vigorous new management worked hard to improve services and win back customers.

In recent years Stagecoach Western Buses has played a key role in providing south-west Scotland with a modern, high-quality transport system. Substantial investment has been made in new buses, ranging from low-floor Dennis Darts which are accessible to baby buggies and wheelchair passengers, through to high-capacity articulated express coaches, a type pioneered in Britain by Stagecoach. These have helped in the development of new express services.

In the leisure market the company has successfully launched open-top tours of some of the most popular places in its territory, such as Arran and Bute. And working with local authorities and the government's Rural Transport Fund, it has introduced new routes to serve some of the more remote communities in south-west Scotland.

Stagecoach is a Scottish company and one of the world's biggest transport providers, with bus and coach operations in the USA, Hong Kong, Australia and New Zealand, as well as throughout Britain. Among its other interests are rail and tram operations.

This volume, however, concentrates on the role of Stagecoach Western Buses in serving south-west Scotland, and on the company's distinguished heritage. The pages which follow illustrate how vehicles have been transformed over the years, from primitive solid-tyred charabancs to today's air-suspended buses and coaches - giving the company's customers a higher quality of service now than at any time in the past.

Graeme Torrance
Managing Director,
Stagecoach West Scotland

By the mid-1930s Western was running around 50 double-deckers. It expanded its fleet in the second half of the decade and did this partly by purchasing second-hand Leyland Titans. This Leyland-bodied TD1 in Ayr had been new to Southdown Motor Services in 1930. It was one of 23 bought by Western in 1935.
Garry Ward collection.

THE ROOTS OF Stagecoach Western Buses are to be found in the creation in 1932 of the Western SMT Co Ltd - but Western SMT had two main forerunners which sowed the seed for what became for a time Scotland's biggest bus company.

First was the Scottish General Transport Co, formed in 1913 by the London-based British Electric Traction (BET) group, which was primarily a tramcar operator and whose Scottish interests included the Rothesay Tramways Co. In Scotland BET operated a small number of buses to provide feeder services to its tramway operations in the Airdrie and Greenock areas, as well as developing new services in places like Ardrossan, Largs and Dunoon. Expansion of its bus operations came after the end of the Great War, and this included the establishment of services in Ayrshire and Renfrewshire which were operated under the Scottish Transport name.

And secondly there was Midland Bus Services, based in Airdrie, which had been set up after the war by John Sword. Sword was typical of many servicemen

demobilised at the end of the World War I who saw a future in mechanised transport - but he had a rather grander vision than most of his compatriots.

The war had hastened vehicle development and improved reliability. It had also helped create a new generation of motor mechanics with the skills to keep temperamental early motor vehicles on the road. This combination of better vehicles and skilled men to drive and maintain them opened up a wealth of new opportunities.

By the mid-1920s Midland was running from Glasgow to towns on the Ayrshire coast in competition with Scottish Transport, and in 1928 it reached south to Stranraer and Dumfries - a significant achievement at a time when pneumatic tyres were still something of a novelty and dual-carriageway roads were far in the future.

The buses were primitive, with petrol engines and, initially, solid tyres. They had high-frame chassis which were basically the same as those used for lorries of the time. That was something which was changing in the late 1920s, as

Solid tyres and a body whose design clearly owes something to Edwardian tramcars characterised buses of the mid-1920s. This is a 1924 Leyland SG with Leyland-built bodywork licensed to carry 39 seated passengers. It carries destination boards for the service between Kilmarnock and Troon via Dundonald. Bus design was advancing rapidly at this time and this Scottish Transport Leyland, and others like it, only operated for five or six years. *SJB collection*

leading manufacturers such as Leyland and AEC recognised that the growing demand for bus travel justified the design of purpose-built bus and coach chassis which would offer better ride quality.

BET's Scottish Transport, which moved its headquarters from Bothwell to Kilmarnock in 1924, had a network of routes heading west to the coast and north to Glasgow. In 1929 it followed Midland into the far south-west with a service to Stranraer, operated jointly with the Caledonian Omnibus Co of Dumfries. The company also had a substantial presence on the south bank of the River Clyde, and in

...929 buses operated by its ...reenock Motor Services ...bsidiary replaced trams in ...reenock and Port Glasgow. ...cottish Transport's offices were ...cated above the company's bus ...ation in Kilmarnock's Portland ...treet. This was the first purpose-...uilt enclosed bus station in ...cotland, and one of the first ...nywhere in Britain. The ...ompany's main garage was ...stablished at Nursery Avenue in ...ilmarnock, and part of the site ...as still in use by Stagecoach ...estern Buses over 70 years later.

By the end of the 1920s ...lidland and Scottish Transport ...ere the major operators to the ...outh-west of Glasgow, a position ...chieved partly by introducing new ...ervices and partly by acquiring the ...usinesses of many of the small ...us operators which had been ...stablished after the Great War. ...lowever change was in the air.

Throughout Britain the rapid ...xpansion of bus services was ...itting the railway companies' ...onopoly of transport outside

urban areas. And competition between bus companies was largely unregulated and often fierce. Stories of buses racing to be the first at stops to pick up passengers abounded, and accidents - fortunately minor - were not uncommon.

The government stepped in. To aid the railway companies it gave them powers in 1928 to operate buses, which most of them exercised by buying a stake in established bus companies, although a few operated their own bus fleets for a short period, including the London Midland and Scottish which from 1929 had a fleet of 10 Albion buses and coaches based in Largs. And it introduced a system of licensing which imposed tight controls over routes, timetables and fares. This introduced a measure of stability to bus operation, and the controls set up by the 1930 Road Traffic Act would remain in force with relatively little change until 1986.

Against this background, major changes took place in the

The LMS Railway commenced operations between Greenock and Largs in March 1929 using Albion PM28s such as this, with 32-seat LMSR-built body. It was one of eight similar buses which were acquired by SMT in November 1931 when it absorbed the business of Gourock Pullman Services. The Gourock company had in late 1929 come under the joint control of the LMS and Scottish General's Greenock Motor Services subsidiary. *Robert Grieves collection*

ownership of Scotland's buses. In 1931 BET sold Scottish Transport, which ran around 225 buses, to the Scottish Motor Traction Co of Edinburgh, which had been set up in 1905. Scottish Transport was renamed Western SMT in June 1932. SMT was part-owned by two of the big railway companies, the LMS and LNER, and had acquired John Sword's Midland Bus Services in 1929. The 200-strong Midland fleet was added to that of the new Western SMT company,

An early version of the Western SMT name seen on an Albion Valiant delivered in 1932, the year of the company's formation. The stylish 30-seat body was by Burlingham. Note the curtains and the roof-mounted luggage rack with access steps above the rear wheel. *Robert Grieves collection*

with John Sword taking over as Western's general manager. Other smaller businesses were acquired too, including in 1932 Ayr & District, which ran 50 buses, mostly of AEC manufacture, and Ayrways Motor Services, running a dozen small buses, mainly Guys.

The new Western SMT company was now running 500 buses, making it one of Scotland's biggest bus businesses.

The company's position in Ayr had also been strengthened. At the start of 1932 a fleet of 31 new SMT Leyland Titan double-deck buses replaced Ayr Corporation's electric trams, which had been operating since 1901.

At the same time SMT also took over the operation of Ayrshire's only other municipal transport undertaking, buying Kilmarnock

New deliveries to Western in 1932-33 included 30 Gilford 168OTs with Wycombe bodies, none of which operated for longer than seven years. The vertical cylinders visible below the headlamps were an early form of air suspension. *Robert Grieves collection*

Corporation's fleet of 19 single-deck buses. Kilmarnock Corporation had introduced bus services in 1924 as it started to replace its ailing and unprofitable tramcars after just 20 years of operation. The first trams had run in 1904; the last was withdrawn in 1926 - a short life for a tramway system. Responsibility for both the Ayr and Kilmarnock operations passed to Western SMT in July 1932.

Another tramway featured in Western's early history - on the isle of Bute. The Rothesay Tramways Co had started operating horse-drawn trams in 1882, and in 1902 BET took over and replaced horse power with electricity. The line which connected Rothesay with nearby Port Bannatyne was then extended across the island to Ettrick

Bay in 1905. The sale of BET's Scottish Transport buses to SMT in 1931 included the Rothesay Tramways Co and the associated McKirdy and McMillan business which claimed to have introduced the first motor bus to Bute as early as 1909.

The two Rothesay businesses were under Western's control from 1932. The tram line was closed in 1936, at which time Rothesay Tramways absorbed the McKirdy and McMillan business and then continued as a bus operator until being absorbed by Western in 194 at which time it was running 24 buses including nine double-deckers. By then the only other operator on the island was Yates of Rothesay, who operated a circular route to Canada Hill. Yeats was later acquired by McGill's of

Barrhead who operated on Bute under the rather grand title of Rothesay Motor Services. These operations - but not the vehicles - were taken over by Western in 1965.

For most of the 1930s Western was the main operator in central Ayrshire, with networks of local services in the Ayr and Kilmarnock areas, and through services north to Glasgow and south to Galloway. From Glasgow it ran local services south to Newton Mearns, Mearnskirk and Neilston, and west to Greenock and Gourock. It also ran from Glasgow to Airdrie, Longriggend and Bathgate, but that operation, which had been part of Midland Bus Services, and 30 buses, was transferred to the Edinburgh-based SMT company in 1935. However, Western buses could still be seen in Airdrie on a cross-country route from Ayr, previously operated by Currie and Thomson of Calderbank. for the following three decades.

Long-distance coach services linked Glasgow with London and with major towns in Lancashire. The Lancashire services had been developed by Scottish Transport in conjunction with sister BET company Ribble Motor Services.

Initially the company's buses were blue (a colour used by SMT), but from 1934 a distinctive white and black livery was adopted, with the Western fleetname in shaded gold block letters. This style of name was remarkably long-lived, surviving until 1978.

The 1930s were good years for the bus industry and Western invested in new vehicles and new premises. It bought Gilford coaches in the early 1930s, taking over 50 between 1932 and 1934, as well as a couple of rare double-deck buses from the same maker. But it was Leyland which became the company's major supplier. The first double-deckers for Scottish Transport had been Leyland Titans in 1928. Titan double-deckers and the equivalent Tiger single-deckers would feature in Western's new vehicle purchases in most years until 1939, and were often supplemented by canny purchases of second-hand examples, usually from major English fleets.

There were a few unusual Leylands in the fleet, including a three-axle Titanic double-decker which with 72 seats was Scotland's biggest bus - setting a record which would remain unbroken until the late 1950s. It had been bought by

In 1935 Western bought 29 Leyland Tiger TS7s with handsome Leyland bodies featuring art-deco styling details on the window pillars. These 30-seat buses had a sliding section in the roof and a large luggage rack at the rear. The majority of these buses were rebuilt as double-deckers in 1944-45. *SJB collection*

Midland in 1928 and operated for Western until 1946, often on the busy Glasgow to Ayr service. There were also 21 three-axle Tiger single-deckers bought in 1935 which were not a success. They were returned to their manufacturer in 1938 - and at a time when most redundant three-year-old buses should have easily found new buyers were actually re-purchased by Western for spare parts. The advantage of using three axles was that it allowed the overall length of the bus to be increased to 30ft from the maximum of 27ft 6in which was permitted on conventional two-axle buses. This in turn increased passenger capacity.

Western also took one large batch of Leyland Cheetahs. The lightweight Cheetah in theory offered lower running costs and, because its smaller engine was shorter than the unit used in the

A new fleetname appeared in 1936, as seen on this Leyland Titan TD4 photographed at Leyland prior to delivery. There were 25 buses in this batch, most of which were fitted with new Northern Counties bodies in 1949-50 and served the company until 1960. *Leyland*

Tiger, also offered increased space for passengers. Forty Cheetahs delivered in 1936 had 37-seat bodywork - only one fewer than the unsuccessful three-axle Tigers and two more than a conventional two-axle Tiger. The Cheetahs may, of course, have been false economy and proved to be troublesome in service. Most were withdrawn in 1944-45 after less than 10 years' service, whereas a batch of Titan double-deckers purchased at the same time served the company for almost 25 years after being fitted with new bodywork in 1949.

Touring and private hire work was covered in the late 1930s by Bedford WTBs with Duple bodies. Western had a limited touring programme which included destinations such as the Wye Valley and Devon and Cornwall.

For its Glasgow to London service Western was running petrol-engined Gilfords in the early 1930s, replacing them with diesel-engined Leyland Tigers from 1935. Diesels offered greater reliability and much improved fuel economy, although with the trade-off of more noise and less refinement. In fact the London run had seen some pioneering work with diesel power as early as 1932 when Midland introduced two diesel-engined AEC Regals to the service. Bear in mind that the Glasgow to London express had only started in 1928, and that a few years before that the solid-tyred charabanc was considered the ultimate in luxury. The rapid development in coach design was nothing short of

remarkable. By 1938 Western was running Leyland Tiger TS7s with fully-fronted Burlingham bodies on the London service.

The outbreak of war in 1939 brought changes to Western, as to all bus companies. Leisure travel would soon be curtailed, and express services suspended for the duration of hostilities. The key demand on bus companies was to provide transport for the country's workforce. Up until 1939 Western had in the main been buying single-deck buses and coaches. Out of a fleet numbering some 475 vehicles in 1939, around two-thirds were single-deckers. That was about to change.

The allocation of new buses during the war years was under the control of the Ministry of War Transport, and Western started to get new vehicles from 1942

beginning with more Leyland Titans which were soon followed by two marques which were new to the company - Guy and Daimler. These were accompanied by Bedford OWB single-deckers. In addition Western, along with other SMT group companies, had many of its prewar Tiger single-deckers rebodied as double-deckers. Between 1943 and 1945 almost 50 Western Tigers dating from between 1935 and 1939 were fitted with new double-deck bodies by Alexander of Stirling (another SMT group company) to boost the fleet's passenger capacity. As built the Tigers were typically 32-seaters; after rebodying they were 53-seaters.

The company's distinctive black and white livery changed too with new buses and wartime repaints being grey.

For many years this 72-seat Leyland Titanic was Scotland's biggest bus. It was new in 1927 and had a Leyland body and had originally been a Leyland demonstrator. It operated for Midland from 1928, and passed to Western SMT in 1932. It ran for Western until 1946. *Robert Grieves collection*

THE END OF the war saw Western facing new challenges. Demand for public transport was reaching unprecedented levels. The company still had a few vehicles in service dating back to 1930 and was keen to modernise its fleet. And British vehicle manufacturers were being urged to export, while at the same time they were getting record orders from home-based customers.

With demand for new buses outstripping supply, Western placed orders for new vehicles with AEC, Daimler and Guy, as well as with its main prewar supplier Leyland. Some of these manufacturers were to fare better than others in Western's future orders. The last new AECs entered service in 1951, as did the last Daimlers (until 1965, at any rate). Guy did rather better, supplying double-deckers, albeit in small quantities, until 1956 and single-deckers, also in small numbers, until 1960. Leyland re-emerged as the company's preferred supplier, and Leylands would feature prominently in Western's new bus and coach orders right through to 1984.

Glasgow-built Albions appeared too, with a batch of Venturer double-deckers in 1949.

Slow deliveries of new buses saw the extensive modernisation of some old ones. To re-launch the Glasgow to London service in 1946 the company bought thirty 12-year-old Leyland Lions - most coming from sister company Central SMT - and had them fitted with new Leyland engines and gearboxes, and new 30-seat coach bodies by Brush of Loughborough. These were stop-gaps, and their replacement started in 1948 with the delivery of new Leyland Tigers with Burlingham coach bodies.

The postwar Labour government was committed to nationalisation of public transport, and this saw Western become part of the new state-owned British Transport Commission (BTC) in 1949 (although the purchase was back-dated to April 1948), along with the SMT group's other bus-operating companies. This was to bring yet more change.

Indeed change had already started in 1945 when Western acquired Dunlop of Greenock, which operated a popular service to Largs. This ran as a separate subsidiary with 28 buses until 1949 when it was integrated into the main fleet at the same time as the 111-bus Greenock Motor Services, the former Scottish Transport

subsidiary which had been under SMT or Western control for 20 years.

A direct result of the creation of BTC was Western's take-over at the start of 1950 of the Dumfries-based Caledonian Omnibus Co. This had been part of the Tilling group, which operated bus services in England and Wales, and which had also been taken over by BTC. It was the Tilling group's only Scottish business, and it made sense to have it managed in Scotland. Caledonian's services covered the south-west corner of the country from Stranraer to Dumfries, and south across the border to Carlisle. It also had services to Edinburgh, these were operated by SMT and Western. Caledonian operated 138 buses which included Scotland's biggest fleet of Dennises (36) and of Bristols (18). Dennises had been Caledonian's preferred chassis during the 1930s, but as a Tilling company its postwar purchases were all Bristols with Eastern Coach Works bodies; both these

In 1946 Western took 40 AEC Regals with neat 36-seat Burlingham bodies. Twelve - including this bus turning on to Jamaica Bridge in Glasgow - were rebodied as double-deckers in the mid-1950s. *Robert Grieves collection*

manufacturers were Tilling-owned. Most of the Caledonian company's double-deckers were elderly TD1 Titans, but it did have four modern Bristol Ks, the only postwar Ks supplied new to a Scottish company.

Further expansion by Western quickly followed, with the acquisition of two associated Paisley-based companies, Young's Bus Service and the Paisley & District Omnibus Co. Between them they ran almost 140 vehicles, most of which were double-deckers. The two companies ran an extensive network of local services in Paisley, as well as trunk routes through to Glasgow and down to the Clyde coast at Largs.

Western SMT had now reached its peak in terms of territory served. It was the major operator in an area from the Clyde to the Solway, with routes to every major town and village west of the main A74 road which it used for its express services from Glasgow to London and Lancashire. And it served Bute. Its fleet in the mid-1950s totalled 1,100 vehicles with double-deckers predominating - there were over 750. New depots were built to replace existing but inadequate facilities in Ayr, Cumnock and Greenock.

It was a mixed fleet. Caledonian had operated Bedfords, Bristols, Leylands and Dennises, along with a few AECs. The Paisley companies ran Albions, Daimlers, Guys, Leylands, Maudslays and a few

Bedford coaches. Western itself had been buying AECs, Albions, Daimlers, Guys and Leylands.

The end of the war brought a change of colours too. The prewar black and white scheme was retained for coaches, but buses were painted in a new livery: red and cream. The block capital Western name was retained on buses, but for coaches a stylish new script-style name was introduced.

A programme of modernising pre-war buses was continuing, and while relatively few second-hand buses joined the fleet after World War II, the company did have an eye for the occasional bargain. So when London Transport started selling off its wartime utility Guy Arabs, Western was a ready buyer. It took 22 in 1951 and a further 43 in 1953-54. Some were rebodied, others simply refurbished and repainted. The last and most extensively rebuilt examples - which were fitted with new Northern Counties bodies and concealed radiators - survived until 1967, although all the unrebuilt buses had been withdrawn by 1959.

The adoption of horizontal underfloor engines by most of the major manufacturers of single-deck chassis at the start of the 1950s created a new generation of modern-looking vehicles with higher seating capacities, and rendered the previous half-cab models obsolete - almost overnight in the case of coaches.

Two Albion Valiants delivered

in 1951 had the distinction of being the last front-engined half-cab single-deckers bought by Western, and were quickly followed by the company's first underfloor-engined coaches which entered service in the summer of 1951. These were 14 AEC Regal IVs with 30-seat Alexander bodies with toilets and were used to counter competition from a new operator on the Glasgow-London route, Northern Roadways, which was using similar vehicles with hostesses on board. The Regal IVs had been diverted from an SMT order to give Western new coaches quickly, and they were to be the company's last AECs.

From 1952 the standard coaches on the London services were Guy Arabs with stylish centre-entrance Alexander bodies. The centre entrance layout meant that there were two seats up front alongside the driver, giving a pair of lucky passengers an unrivalled view of the road ahead. The centre door layout was briefly popular on mid-engined coaches in the early 1950s but had one drawback in that the driver couldn't help passengers off the coach (and collect their tips at the end of a trip!) - as they would already be alighting before he could get out of his seat. From 1954 Western's new coaches were all of front entrance design.

The licensing system which had been set up by the 1930 Road Traffic Act allowed what could be described as controlled competition, and while Western provided a comprehensive network of services from Renfrewshire in the north to Dumfriesshire in the south, there were other operators in the region. In Ayrshire three co-operatives, AA, A1 and Clyde Coast, provided services in an area stretching broadly from Largs in the north to Ayr in the south, and inland to Kilmarnock. And in the Paisley area

It's June 1950, six months after Western had taken over Caledonian, but there's no sign of the change on this 1928 Titan TD1 with 1947 Croft body which still carries the Caledonian name and fleet number. The Western office, just visible on the right, is offering a Grand Mystery Tour for 2s (10p). *A B Cross*

Western shared the town's local services with four family-run businesses, McGill's, Paton, Cunningham and Graham's, plus a fifth - Smith's - which was owned by the Scottish Co-operative Wholesale Society. These operators gained greater prominence as their operations expanded after Glasgow Corporation withdrew its tram services from Paisley, Barrhead and Renfrew in 1957.

The nationalisation of the Tilling group of bus companies had brought with them into state ownership the two associated manufacturers - Bristol and Eastern Coach Works. As a result of nationalisation their products were available only to state-owned companies which, of course, now included Western. Consequently from 1955 Bristol Lodekkas started to appear in the Western fleet. For the following ten years double-deck bus orders would be shared between Bristol and Leyland, while for coach operation Bristol would gradually oust Guy.

With an eye to improving passenger comfort on busy long-distance services many new double-deckers from 1956 had doors on the rear platform, operated by the conductor - or, more often, conductress. However as bus design evolved, the company switched to forward entrances on double-deckers in 1962, taking the new high-capacity (70-seat) Bristol Lodekka FLF-series and a new and untried model from the Leyland group, the Albion Lowlander.

To minimise the overall height of its double-deckers and thus allow greater operational flexibility, all of those ordered in the late 1940s and early 1950s were of lowbridge layout, with the upper-deck gangway running along the offside of the bus. This gave access to bench seats for four passengers. The layout was inconvenient for travellers in the top deck, and the gangway intruded into the lower saloon - with most buses carrying a warning - Mind your head - to passengers travelling on the seats on the offside of the lower deck.

The Bristol Lodekka used a drop-centre rear axle and an offset drive-shaft to lower the floor level in the lower deck and to thus provide a conventional centre gangway on both decks while still maintaining a low overall height of around 13ft 6in - the same as a lowbridge bus. The Lowlander, assembled at the Albion factory in Scotstoun, was Leyland's answer to the lowbridge problem, and used the same Leyland O.600 engine as the Titan PD2 and PD3, a type of which Western had over 300 in operation.

Yet the Lowlander proved to be a troublesome vehicle, and within four years Western was starting to dispose of some of its fleet to sister companies in what was now known as the Scottish Bus Group (SBG). Western had been the biggest buyer of the Albion Lowlander - it purchased 111 in total between 1962 and 1965.

New Guy Arabs featured in Western's purchases from 1942 to 1960. This Arab III was one of seven delivered in 1953 which were the first in the company to feature new-look fronts in place of the traditional exposed radiator which had characterised previous double-deck deliveries. They had 53-seat Northern Counties bodies. *SJB collection*

When its last six Lowlanders entered service in 1965, they did so alongside the first of a new generation of rear-engined double-deckers. These were Daimler Fleetlines - marking a return to a manufacturer who had last supplied new buses to Western in 1951. They had stylish Alexander bodies seating 75 - a figure which finally overtook Western's high-capacity Titanic which had been Scotland's biggest bus three decades earlier. Even bigger buses soon followed, when seven 83-seat Daimler Fleetlines were introduced to Paisley in 1967 for use on a busy local service. These were 33ft-long, compared with the standard figure of 31ft, and once again gave Western the distinction of operating Scotland's biggest buses.

Between 1955 and 1957 Western bought 107 leyland Titan PD2s, with bodywork by Northern Counties or, as on this bus, Alexander. Most of the PD2s were 59-seaters. From 1958 the company chose the longer PD3 model which seated 67. *SJB*

The Fleetline became Western's standard double-decker. However rear-engined buses were more complex and less reliable than the established front-engined models they were replacing, and by the start of the 1970s Western - along with most other SBG companies - was only buying double-deckers where their high seating capacity was absolutely necessary. Western did try an alternative to the Fleetline in the shape of the rear-engined Bristol VRT which had succeeded the Lodekka. It proved even more unreliable and after just three years in service all were disposed of, with the vast majority going to English fleets in exchange for trusty Lodekkas.

The answer to double-deck unreliability was to switch to single-deckers. For most routes Western started buying Leyland Leopards with Alexander Y-type bodies which had 49 high-backed seats for longer-distance services c 53 bus seats for shorter routes. The 53-seaters could - in theory at leas - carry 24 standing passengers. This gave a total carrying capacity not far short of that offered by the Fleetlines, and higher than the older double-deckers they were replacing, albeit at the expense of passenger comfort in busy periods. The first Y-type Leopards were delivered in 1963, and between 1971 to 1979 the vast majority of Western's new buses were of this type.

From 1962 Western specified forward-entrance double-deckers. This Bristol Lodekka with 70-seat ECW body was one of 26 delivered that year.
Iain MacGregor

The Albion Lowlander succeeded the Leyland Titan in Western's orders from 1962. This 1963 bus, seen in Irvine, has a 71-seat Alexander body.
Iain MacGregor

For a time Western operated Scotland's biggest buses - seven 83-seat Daimler Fleetlines. This one has bodywork by Northern Counties.
John Burnett

In the 1960s Western was still running over 1,000 buses, of which almost 800 were double-deckers. The route network and the area served remained pretty much as in 1950, and while there was modest expansion, the company was facing the twin problems of increasing costs and decreasing passenger numbers - problems which bedevilled the bus industry right through the 1960s and 1970s.

A limited extended tours programme to destinations such as Devon and the Scottish Highlands survived into the 1960s, principally operated by Guy LUFs in the black-and-white coach livery. Popular day and afternoon excursion programmes continued too, along with a considerable amount of private hire work.

Modest expansion in the mid-1960s saw Western take over the business of J Clark & Sons of Dumfries in 1965. Clark ran a service to Glencaple and two elderly buses were taken over by Western and immediately sold. Some journeys from Kirkcudbright to Borgue were also introduced to replace a service which had been operated by Campbell of Gatehouse.

The operations of R Murray & Sons of Stranraer were acquired in January 1966. Murray operated seven vehicles, none of which were taken over by Western. Later in the same year Garnock Valley Motors ceased operation of its hourly service between Kilbirnie and Beith. Most of the route was already covered by through services operated by Western, but the company added some peak-hour journeys to cover the former Garnock Valley route. In 1968 SCWS subsidiary Smith of Barrhead gave up its services from Paisley to Todholm and South Nitshill. Smith's fleet of eight double-deckers was a modern one, and included four Leyland Titans similar to many already being operated by Western - but all were sold without being used.

The move towards single-deckers at the end of the 1960s coincided with growing interest in one-man-operation of urban bus services. Limited one-man-operation of single-deckers started in 1967, with the first one-man double-deckers following towards the end of 1968. The aim in dispensing with the services of conductors was two-

On a wet day at the junction of the Carrick Castle road with the main A83 from Glasgow to Campbeltown - the spot known generally as Rest and be Thankful - mail is unloaded from a Leyland Leopard bound for Tarbert and transferred to an ex-MacBrayne Bedford VAS1, one of four MacBrayne vehicles acquired by Western in 1970. These non-standard buses enjoyed reasonable lives with Western; the last two were not withdrawn until 1980. SJB

fold - to reduce costs and to alleviate a perpetual shortage of staff which was affecting service reliability. It would gradually be spread company-wide, with the last conductress hanging up her ticket machine at Greenock depot in 1981 - although conductor operation would reappear briefly in the late 1980s on ex-London Transport Routemasters in Glasgow.

Over the years Western had been attracted to the economy and durability of Gardner engines. These were specified in Guy Arabs and Bristol Lodekkas in the 1950s, and in Daimler Fleetlines and Bristol VRTs in the 1960s. However Leyland's chassis were only available with Leyland engines, and SBG convinced

14

Seddon, a truck maker who was a relatively minor player in the bus business, to produce what was in effect the equivalent of a Leopard but with a Gardner engine, the Pennine VII. Western took 213 between 1975 and 1980.

Continuing concern about the unreliability of rear-engined buses saw SBG collaborate with Ailsa Trucks, the Barrhead-based importer of Swedish-built Volvo trucks, to produce a new front-engined double-deck chassis, the Ailsa. Western added 34 Ailsas to its fleet between 1978 and 1980, and also took its last Fleetlines in the same period. It then turned to Dennis for the supply of new buses.

The company's territory expanded in unlikely directions in the 1970s. First, it reached down the Mull of Kintyre to Campbeltown on Loch Fyne, and north to Oban from Ardrishaig, when it took over bus services previously operated by David MacBrayne, whose bus and coach business was being absorbed by SBG. It also introduced new express services linking Glasgow with Londonderry, Letterkenny and Bundoran. These were operated jointly with Ulsterbus and, for Letterkenny, with the Londonderry & Lough Swilly Railway.

Other developments in the 1970s included the launch in 1977 of an express service from Linwood to Glasgow via the M8 motorway, operated jointly with Graham's Bus Services. And in 1978 a rural transport initiative saw a service running under the RUTEX banner from Dalmellington to New Cumnock, and onward to Ballochmyle Hospital for the benefit of visitors.

Western strengthened its position in Paisley in 1979 by taking over the businesses of Paton Bros of Renfrew and Cunningham's Bus Service of Paisley. Most of the 35 buses acquired with these two companies were quickly sold, but 10 modern Leopards from the Paton fleet were retained and five of these were allocated to a new operation on Islay where Western had established a base following the collapse of the previous operator.

The company's fleetname - unchanged on buses since 1934 - was revised in 1978 as SBG adopted a new corporate look which saw the company start trading as Western Scottish. Buses on the two islands served by the company adopted the style Bute Western Scottish and Islay Western Scottish.

The early 1980s saw Western adding new types of vehicle to its fleet. The last of a long line of Leyland Leopards with Alexander Y-type bodies were delivered in 1980, along with the last Fleetlines. It switched to Dennis Dominators for its double-deck orders, and to Leyland Tigers and Dennis Dorchesters for its single-deck requirements. These brought a new bodybuilder to the fleet, Plaxton.

In the early 1980s SBG carried out a massive examination of its services under an exercise known as ScotMAP - MAP standing for Market Analysis Project. This saw many routes being revised and vehicle requirements being re-evaluated. For Western it marked a decline in its requirement for double-deck buses and the 24 Ailsas delivered in 1980 marked the last big intake of new double-deckers. Its next double-deckers came from London Transport in the shape of 32 six-year-old Fleetlines purchased between 1981 and 1983.

Express services operated in Scotland by SBG companies were relaunched under the Scottish Citylink brand in October 1983, largely as a response to the growing competition being experienced following the deregulation of coach operations in 1980. Western had launched its own network of local express services under the Cityliner name, operating from Ayr, New Cumnock, Wemyss Bay and Kilmacolm to Glasgow, and from Ayr to Greenock using the Coastliner name. These were generally operated by new Plaxton-bodied Dennis Dorchesters.

Western's traditional holiday services to Lancashire's coastal resorts had been speeded up as the motorway system developed, and in the 1980s new destinations further afield were served - for example Bournemouth and Bideford.

Twenty new Plaxton-bodied Tiger coaches in 1984 were delivered in Citylink blue and yellow, rather than in Western's black and white livery - and were to be Western's last new Leylands. They were unusual in having Gardner 6HLXCT engines instead of the standard Leyland TL11H. Having lost business to Gardner-engined Seddon Pennines in the

Front-engined Ailsas with Alexander bodies were bought by Western in 1978 and 1980. *John Burnett*

1970s and to Gardner-powered Dennis Dorchesters at the start of the 1980s, Leyland had re-engineered its Tiger chassis to accommodate the Gardner engine. More unusual coaches in Citylink colours in 1984 were three MCW Metroliner 69-seat double-deckers. The launch of Citylink saw new services being introduced, such as the X12 which provided a new link between Glasgow Airport, Paisley, East Kilbride, Hamilton and Edinburgh, and which Western operated jointly with Central Scottish.

Coaches on the London service initially remained in the blue and white Scottish livery introduced in 1976, but this operation adopted Citylink branding from 1985.

In an attempt to encourage rail use the Galloway Rail-Link service was introduced in 1984. This involved Western, British Rail and Dumfries and Galloway council and it saw through tickets being made available for bus-rail journeys with passengers changing mode at Dumfries station.

There was growing interest in making public transport accessible to disabled people, and in 1984 Western was among the first companies in Scotland to operate coaches adapted to carry wheelchairs. The vehicles used were existing Seddon Pennines with 49-seat Alexander T-type bodies. The conversion was carried out at the company's Nursery Avenue workshops in Kilmarnock and involved fitting a wheelchair lift on the nearside just ahead of the rear wheels, with doors in the body side which allowed the wheelchair to be rolled straight into the coach.

Tracking was fitted to the floor to provide secure anchorage points and in their new form the coaches had 24 seats and space for up to six wheelchairs. As well as converting vehicles for its own use, Western carried out similar rebuilds for other SBG companies.

At the end of the decade Western would become involved in providing regular bus services aimed at disabled travellers, operating dial-a-ride services in Ayr, Irvine and Kilmarnock on behalf of the Strathclyde Passenger Transport Executive and using Talbot Freeway minibuses.

Western's Volvos with Alexander M-type bodies ended their days in Scottish Citylink colours. When new they had carried the company's distinctive black and white coach livery, as shown on page 35. *John Burnett*

After buying former London Transport buses in the early 1950s, 30 years later ex-London buses appeared in the Western fleet once more, with the purchase of 17 Daimler Fleetlines with MCW bodies. This one is seen in Cumnock bus station in 1985. *SJB*

Western's last new Northern Counties bodies in the Scottish Bus Group era were delivered on Daimler Fleetlines in 1979. This one is promoting the company's Glasgow to London Service. *John Burnett*

Dennis Dorchesters were introduced to the coach fleet in 1983, with Plaxton Paramount bodies. Before adopting the Scottish Citylink name, Western used Cityliner branding for some of its express services, as seen on this coach in Largs. It was one of the company's first Dorchesters and introduced modern Plaxton coachwork to the fleet. *SJB*

Among the most unusual double-deckers operated by Western were two Volvo Citybuses with Alexander RDC coach bodies. This example, seen leaving Glasgow for Ayr, is in the company's black, grey, red and white colours with the retro-style Western Scottish fleetname which harked back to the long-lived block-lettered name used from 1936 to 1979. It had previously operated in Citylink livery. *SJB*

IN 1985 THE government introduced a new Transport Act. Its aim was to free bus operators from the strict licensing control which had been in place for over 50 years and which was no longer appropriate in an industry where the key issue was not competition, but a steady decline in the number of people travelling by bus. This was in turn leading to increased levels of subsidy to keep bus services running, especially in rural areas. By deregulating local bus services the Transport Act intended to stimulate competition from new operators, reduce subsidy, and open up the bus business to new ideas.

And at the same time as deregulating the industry, the government wanted buses to be run by the private sector. This meant that the Scottish Bus Group was to be privatised - which marked the first step in creating today's Stagecoach Western Buses.

SBG responded to the changes by redrawing the boundaries of its subsidiary companies, and splitting the biggest into smaller, more manageable, units. For Western,

the biggest company with over 650 buses, this meant the loss of its routes in Renfrewshire and North Ayrshire. Seven depots - at Greenock, Inchinnan, Johnstone, Largs, Paisley, Rothesay and Thornliebank - with 334 buses were taken over by a new company, Clydeside Scottish.

Western retained 319 buses and the depots at Ayr, Carlisle, Cumnock, Dumfries, Girvan, Kilmarnock and Stranraer. Its main area of operation was broadly south of a line drawn from Kilmarnock to Irvine. The Islay operations, set up in 1979, were transferred to Midland Scottish, along with Western's Ardrishaig base inherited from MacBrayne in 1970. The old-established Bute services were taken over by Clydeside.

These changes were implemented in June 1985. As part of the change the company had been renamed. As a former BET subsidiary, Western was the only SBG company to have its registered office in London (at 298 Regent Street, where it had a travel office) and its name was changed

in February 1985 from Western SMT Co Ltd to Western Scottish Ltd. The other SBG companies were registered in Scotland, where the registrar of companies required that the company names include something more descriptive than just the word Scottish. Consequently the Scottish-registered companies were given names in the style Midland Scottish Omnibuses, and after just three weeks as being plain Western Scottish Ltd, the Western company, too, was brought into line as Western Scottish Omnibuses Ltd on 1 March.

Western had a rethink on its livery in 1985. From 1981 the

black and white coach livery had been altered to include grey stripes whether or not the change was an improvement is open to challenge - and in 1985 the bus livery was changed to black and white with grey stripes. Red relief was added from 1987, and at the same time the Western Scottish name was dropped in favour of an updated version of the traditional style of Western name in capital letters.

The deregulation of local bus services saw a number of new operators appear, many of which were under-funded and short-lived. They created competition not just for Western, but for the other old-established bus businesses in Ayrshire - AA, A1 and Clyde Coast. The uncertainty which deregulation created saw a sudden halt to the purchase of new buses. The only new vehicles in 1984-85 had been coaches. In 1986 no new vehicles joined the fleet.

But some interesting and unusual second-hand ones did. In 1985 SBG had bought the business of Newton of Dingwall, whose fleet included some high-capacity coaches. Five ex-Newton vehicles were bought by Western in 1986. Two were 60-seat Van Hool Astron twin-deck integrals, two were tri-axle Volvo B10MTs with twin-deck 64-seat Plaxton Paramount 4000 bodywork, and the fifth was a Van Hool Alicron integral. The four twin-deck coaches were used on the London service (initially in Newton's livery), while the single-deck Alicron was allocated to a new route linking Stranraer with Dumfries to provide connections with selected London trains. The Van Hools lasted less than 12 months in the fleet, but the Volvos received Citylink colours and saw use on the London service.

Western quickly adapted to the new deregulated market. In Kilmarnock lower fares - promoted as Mad Max - were introduced in 1986 to encourage customer loyalty. And in Ayr in March 1987 Western introduced Scotland's first big conversion of a town's services to high-frequency minibuses when it replaced big buses with 40 new 25-seat Alexander-bodied Dodges marketed as Buzzers. The change typically saw local routes which had been operated by a big bus twice an hour being given a minibus every 10 minutes. Later in the year similar changes were made to town services in Dumfries, using two dozen 12-month-old Mercedes-Benz minibuses bought from sister SBG company Kelvin Scottish.

Other second-hand purchases in 1987 included Fleetlines from elsewhere in SBG - including some with ECW bodies, a combination not previously operated by Western - as well as a small number from West Midlands Travel. In 1988 the company started buying Leyland Nationals from other SBG subsidiaries, initially using them to replace high-floor Leyland Leopards on local services in Ayr and Kilmarnock.

Western's last new double-deckers under SBG ownership were ordered for 1987 delivery. These were to be six mid-engined Volvo Citybuses with Alexander bodywork, but to meet the need for high-capacity vehicles on the Scottish Citylink service between

Glasgow and Edinburgh, two were diverted to Fife Scottish in exchange for a pair of three-year-old Citybuses with rare 70-seat Alexander RDC coach bodies. Of the remaining four new Citybuses, one was fitted out with coach seats to run alongside the ex-Fife coaches on the Citylink service. The other three carried fleet livery.

Deregulation and the competition it created had the side effect of destabilising some businesses. As privatisation loomed, it became apparent that Clydeside was having trouble standing on its own, with its urban services in Greenock and Paisley facing intense competition from other operators, large and small. Western and Clydeside were re-united as one company in May 1989, with a combined fleet of 740 buses and coaches - up from some 650 when the company had been split four years earlier.

While Clydeside had suffered badly from competition, it was more typically small operators who faced serious problems. One such was Dickson of Dumfries which closed without warning in May 1991. Dickson had expanded in the late 1980s, winning contracts for tendered services - often at the expense of Western. Its fleet totalled 35 vehicles, and to provide immediate cover for Dickson's services Western stepped in, reinstating recently-withdrawn buses and buying a model which had never featured in its fleet

The only clue that this is a Western coach lies in the fleet number, L209, alongside the registration plate. This is one of a pair of 60-seat Van Hool Astrons, acquired in 1986 from Newtons of Dingwall. It is seen at Charnock Richard services on the M6, operating on the Glasgow to London service. The high seating capacity was achieved by having a small passenger compartment behind the rear wheels. *SJB*

before: the Leyland Atlantean. In common with other SBG companies Western had bought Daimler Fleetlines rather than Leyland Atlanteans when it switched from front- to rear-engined double-deckers in the mid-1960s. Western's Atlanteans were eight former Greater Manchester examples, all around 12 years old. They were initially operated in their former owner's brown, orange and white colours before being painted in fleet livery.

The privatisation process got off to an uncertain start in 1991 with the likelihood of their being two rival internal bids - one from Western's management and another led by the former Clydeside employees. By this time the fleet had been rationalised to 661 buses operating from 13 depots - Ardrossan, Ayr, Cumnock, Dumfries, Greenock, Inchinnan, Johnstone, Kilmarnock, Largs, Paisley, Rothesay, Stranraer and Thornliebank. The two rival teams reached a compromise and made a joint bid on the basis that if it succeeded the former Clydeside business would immediately be resold to its employees. This duly happened on 14 October 1991, and Western reverted to serving Ayrshire and points south, with through routes to Glasgow. It also

retained the Bute operations, which had been part of Clydeside from 1985 to 1989. The newly independent company - its name soon shortened to Western Scottish Buses Ltd - started off with 332 vehicles.

The company re-evaluated its business. The garage in Ardrossan, which dated back to Scottish Transport days, was closed. In February 1992 it decided to give up its commercial operations in Carlisle. However it expanded in Scotland, starting with a successful bid to run Strathclyde PTE contracted services on Arran in the autumn of 1992, an operation which required 12 buses - nine Leyland Nationals and three Dodge minibuses. The loser on Arran was Arran Transport, and it responded by successfully bidding for SPTE contracts on Bute, where it established a seven-vehicle operation at Western's expense. The battle then spilled over to the Cowal

Western's first Leyland Nationals were 20 Mark 2 models which came from sister SBG company Kelvin Scottish in 1988. This was one of two which had started life with Highland Scottish in 1981. *Garry Ward*

peninsula, where both Western and Arran Transport won SPTE contracts in 1993. Western set up a new operating base in Cowal - som 80 years after its predecessor's first foray into the Dunoon area.

Clyde Coast of Ardrossan introduced local services in Kilmarnock at the start of 1994 in competition with Western. This followed Clyde Coast's acquisition of the Killie Hoppa, a short-lived competitor for Western in the town Western's response was to launch the Coastliner, running over Clyde Coast's old-established route to Largs, but starting from Irvine rather than from Saltcoats, and to transfer some modern Dennis Darts from Ayr to improve its Kilmarnoc services.

Former Greater Manchester Transport Atlanteans, purchased by Western for school contracts in Dumfries & Galloway, ended their days helping out at A1 Service. This bus, with Park Royal body, is in the final version of Western's livery before the Stagecoach takeover - black, two shades of grey and white, with a red band above the lower deck windows. *SJB*

Twelve Dominators delivered in 1983 were Western's first double-deck Dennises. They had Alexander 76-seat bodies. When new they were in the company's established read and cream livery. This late 1980s view in Greenock shows one repainted in the post-1987 black, white, grey and red scheme. *SJB*

Western expanded its double-deck fleet in the late 1980s with second-hand Fleetlines from other Scottish Bus Group companies. This ECW-bodied bus came from Northern Scottish. *John Burnett*

Ten Dennis Darts with Alexander Dash bodies were purchased in 1992. they were diverted from an order being built for Stagecoach.

By the summer of 1995 this Leyland National 2 which Western had bought from Kelvin Scottish in 1988 had been repainted in Stagecoach livery and transferred to the company's new Arran operations. The bus dated from 1981. *Murdoch Currie*

IN COMMON WITH many other bus company management buy-outs in Scotland and England, Western's new owners were struggling to finance fleet replacements. Thanks to a clamp down on investment in the run-up to privatisation, the fleet was older than it would otherwise have been, and this posed a major challenge to its management. On top of that, the company was losing money.

The answer was to sell the company to a group which could invest and build on Western's reputation. Enter Stagecoach, which took over in July 1994.

Stagecoach was, itself, a remarkably young company. It had been set up in 1980 to take advantage of coach deregulation and had successfully introduced express services from Glasgow to Aberdeen, Edinburgh and - in direct competition with Western - London. When England's National Bus Company was privatised, Perth-based Stagecoach had purchased three NBC subsidiaries. It also had small bus operations in Perth and Glasgow, both started up in 1986. In the privatisation of SBG, Stagecoach had been successful in its bid for two companies - Northern Scottish (now Stagecoach Bluebird Buses) and Fife Scottish (now Stagecoach Fife Buses).

After buying Western, Stagecoach immediately set about updating the fleet. The only new vehicles bought by the company during its two-and-a-half years in management ownership had been three Dennis Javelin coaches, a Duple 425 Integral, two Mercedes-Benz minibuses and 10 Dennis Darts which had been diverted from a Stagecoach order. Two Volvo B10M coaches were being fitted with new East Lancs bus bodies when the company changed hands, and were delivered in Stagecoach white in the latter part of 1994.

Stagecoach quickly added 30 new Volvo B6s, followed by 19 Volvo B10M coaches, 38 B10M buses and 45 Mercedes minibuses. In the space of two years the Western fleet was transformed. When Stagecoach took over 50 per cent of the vehicles in the Western fleet were aged 14 years or older. By mid-1997 this figure had been reduced to 33 per cent, and by 1999 was approaching 25 per cent - most of which were school buses.

With the change of ownership came the corporate Stagecoach look, replacing the unusual combination of white, black and grey which, in a variety of layouts, had been the Western fleet livery since 1985.

Under Stagecoach ownership Western has consolidated its position as the leading bus operator in south-west Scotland. The Kilmarnock local service network was quickly improved. Then in October 1994 it bought the bus and coach operations of Arran Transport. This involved 24 vehicles based not just on Arran, but on Bute and in Cowal too, where Western and Arran Transport had been in competition since 1992.

At the start of 1995 Stagecoach took over the operations of A1 Service of Ardrossan, which initially operated as a separate subsidiary under Western management. A1, a cooperative comprising 10 operators running 67 buses, provided services in a triangle bounded by Kilmarnock, Irvine and Ardrossan. Many of its buses were time-expired and Stagecoach immediately replaced much of the fleet with 21 brand-new Volvo Olympians (the biggest single investment in new buses in A1's history), supported by Leyland Titans transferred from its

ondon operations, and Bristol RTs from other group companies. he Titans (many of which were ut into service still in London red) nd the Bristols may not have been ignificantly younger than some of e A1 buses they replaced, but ey were in much better condition. itially the A1 fleet was repainted corporate Stagecoach colours, ut towards the end of 1996 it was ecided to reinstate A1's blue and ream livery for the new Volvo lympians running on the trunk ilmarnock to Ardrossan service.

A Greenock to Ayr service, arketed as Coastline 585, had een introduced by Ashton oaches of Greenock in the ummer of 1994. Over much of its ength - from Largs south - it was ompeting with existing services perated by AA, A1 and Clyde oast. Thus in the summer of 1995 ese three operators plus lydeside pooled their resources to un a competing service, Coastlink 35, in a white and green livery - e colours used by Ashton oaches. A1 used two new Volvo 10Ms with Alexander bodies (and ired two identical vehicles to lyde Coast). Ashton Coaches was uick to complain about the oastlink 535 image adopted by its ompetitors, and this was changed fter a few months to Clyde oaster 535 with a white and red very.

Western took over the ommercial operations of Clyde oast in September 1995, and put em under the control of A1. lyde Coast had earlier withdrawn s local services in Kilmarnock. his made A1 the main operator etween Saltcoats and Largs, and lso the provider of the Largs local ervice. Clyde Coast retained an nterest in the Clyde Coaster 535 ervice until April 1996 when its hare of the operation was taken ver by Western, along with the wo hired Volvo B10Ms. The white

and red Clyde Coaster livery was abandoned in 1999.

During 1996 Western vacated its Nursery Avenue offices, the company's headquarters for some 60 years, and relocated its management to offices at Sandgate in Ayr. At the same time there were some name changes. The company name shrunk yet again, this time to the straightforward Western Buses Ltd, while Stagecoach (A1 Service) Ltd, which had taken over the A1 operations, was renamed A1 Service Ltd. The integration of A1 with Western was completed in the summer of 1997, and the A1 company wound up, although A1 Service was retained as a trading name. The A1 bus terminus - bus station was perhaps too grand a description - in Parkhouse Road, Ardrossan, was closed in 1996 after almost 60 years continuous use.

In June 1997 Western took over AA Buses of Troon, which ran from Ayr to Ardrossan, and locally in Ayr and in Troon. AA Buses ran 30 vehicles, some of which were replaced towards the end of the year by new Dennis Dart SLFs. These were the first low-floor buses purchased by Western, and were operated in AA's green livery. The commercial bus services operated by Shuttle Buses of Kilwinning (established in 1990) were also taken over in 1997. In 1998 Crawford of Neilston gave up

the operation of its limited stop services from Dundonald and Ardrossan to Glasgow, and Western took over. This was followed at the start of 2000 by the Moffat to Dumfries service which had been operated by Gibson of Moffat for over 70 years, leaving Gibson to concentrate on coaching.

The mid-1990s saw Western developing new markets: open-top bus tours and express coach services. Open-top bus services have a long history in sunny south coast English holiday resorts, but were long shunned by Scottish bus companies, not least because of what might generously be described as Scotland's variable climate. Western first introduced open-top buses to Ayr in 1994 on a Burns Heritage Tour which also took in the Butlins Wonderwest Camp. This was followed in the summer of 1995 with the Arran Open Top Experience linking Brodick, Lamlash and Whiting Bay. In 1996 additional services were added on Bute. Dunoon joined the open-top list in 1998, followed by Dumfries and Cumbrae in 1999. All were operated by double-deckers (a first for Arran and Cumbrae). An open-top Leyland Leopard was also used for a season on the Arran Whisky Distillery Tour.

The first of a new generation of express services was launched in December 1994. The X77 ran from

Ayr to Glasgow and was operated by high-quality coaches - Volvo B10Ms with Plaxton Premiere bodies, a vehicle which was to figure prominently on express operations. Subsequent new services included the X75 from Dumfries to Carlisle, operated jointly with Stagecoach Cumberland. A new range of express services was introduced from Annan, Kirkcudbright, Dumfries and Lockerbie via a hub at Moffat to both Glasgow and Edinburgh. Other new routes included the X52 from Ayr to Dalmellington and the X71 from Irvine to Glasgow, both operated hourly. Most of these ventures won new customers for Western, to the extent that on some routes the number of journeys was increased, while on others - starting with the X77 - a new approach was adopted to increasing capacity.

In December 1996 Western took delivery of two articulated Volvo B10Ms with 71-seat Plaxton Premiere bodies. This gave a worthwhile increase of 20 seats over the standard coaches - and turned people's heads. Articulated coaches are rare in Britain, and Western was to become the biggest user with a fleet of 13 in operation by the start of 2000.

Another market which Western explored was the use of dedicated buses for home to school transport. At the start of 1997 it tentatively set up a subsidiary called Schoolbus Ltd, although this never took off. Twelve months later it repainted a Leyland Titan in bright overall yellow to gauge the reaction of local authorities which might have been interested in using buses which were easily identifiable to further the cause of road safety in relation to school children.

In the late 1990s rural transport was recognised by the government as an area needing major investment. A rural transport grant was introduced and Western was among the operators which worked with local authorities to develop new services. These included a quality partnership with Dumfries and Galloway council which saw two fully-accessible Mini Pointer Darts operating from Newton Stewart to small towns and villages on the Machars peninsula. This started in 1999.

At the other extreme Western is also responsible for Stagecoach Glasgow. An initial plan to operate services in Glasgow in late 1994 was dropped when Stagecoach took a minority shareholding in the city' main operator. That was sold in 1996. Stagecoach Glasgow commenced operations in the sprin, of 1997, using the newly-opened M77 motorway to provide fast links between the city centre and suburbs such as Pollok and South Nitshill o, the south-western edge of the city. The services were started with 37 new Volvo single-deckers - most of which were low-floor B6BLEs - and by 2000 Stagecoach Glasgow was running 70 buses.

Clyde Coast

CLYDE COAST was the apt name for a small co-operative running a service along the Clyde from Saltcoats to Largs. For many years this was run by double-deckers. These included distinctive silver-liveried Leyland Titans bought new in the late 1940s, although the vast majority of Clyde Coast's double-deckers over the years were second-hand purchases.

As with other Ayrshire co-operatives, the number of partners fell over time - from four in the 1960s, down to two - Frazer of Fairlie and McGregor of Saltcoats - by the end of the 1970s. In 1987 McGregor took over sole responsibility for the Clyde Coast operation.

The fleet profile changed in the 1970s, as new single-deckers, part-funded by the government's new bus grant, replaced old double-deckers. Double-deck operation ceased in 1972, and Leyland Leopard coaches became the standard vehicles on the service. However the ending of the bus grant in the early 1980s saw Clyde Coast revert to buying second-hand buses and from 1986 these included double-deckers once again.

In 1995 Clyde Coast withdrew from commercial bus operation but continued as an operator of contract services and coaches.

In 1955 Clyde Coast bought this 12-year-old Guy Arab I from Liverpool Corporation. It had a Weymann body and operated until 1959. This is the pier head at Largs. Five similar buses were bought by A1 Service. Clyde Coast's livery at this time was silver with pale blue relief. *S N J White*

A former London Transport RT heads up the Main Street in Largs on its way south to Saltcoats on Clyde Coast's trunk route in 1967. By this time Clyde Coast's buses were blue and grey. *SJB*

In the early 1990s Clyde Coast was running the Largs to Saltcoats service with single-deckers, including this ex-Yorkshire Traction Leyland National. Interestingly the 11.3m-long National seated 52, only four fewer than the RT being used on the service 25 years earlier. *SJB*

Bute

WESTERN HAS BEEN the main bus operator on Bute since 1949 when it absorbed the Rothesay Tramways Company, which had been a subsidiary since 1932. Small bus operators which had primarily been competing with the tramway to Ettrick Bay or providing round-the-island tours were acquired in the early 1930s, giving Rothesay Tramways a virtual monopoly on the island.

The introduction of frequent car ferry services in the 1960s and the rise in car ownership have seen the island's route network gradually cut back over a long period of time.

Double-deck buses were introduced to Bute in 1939 with the arrival of two second-hand 1930 Leyland Titan TD1s which operated for a few months in the summer, and was reintroduced in 1946 with two new Guy Arabs. Double-deckers would be a feature of the island's regular operations until 1971. In 1996 a double-decker re-appeared, with the introduction of summer season tours using an open-top bus.

For ease of maintenance Western tried to keep a fairly standard fleet on Bute from the mid-1950s, initially with batches of Leyland Tiger TS7s and Maudslay Marathons. In the mid 1960s, for example, the double-deckers were all Leyland Titan PD1s, while the single-deckers were Bristol LSs.

The fleet strength at Western's Rothesay depot in the late 1950s was typically around 24, although by the mid-1980s this had fallen to just seven Seddon Pennines. In 2000 Stagecoach Western had a dozen buses based on Bute - an open-top Bristol VRT plus seven Leyland Nationals, three Mercedes-Benz minibuses and a Leyland Leopard coach. These still operated from the original tramway depot at Pointhouse, which is a listed building.

The single-deck fleet in Rothesay in 1965 was made up of Bristol LS6Gs with Alexander bodies - a combination unique to Western. *SJB*

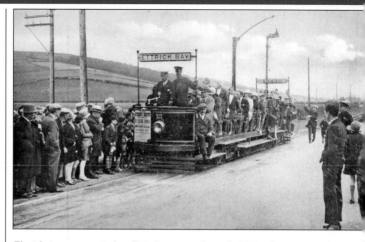

Electric trams operated on Bute from 1902 to 1936. The fleet totalled 21 vehicles.

An early 1950s view of an ex-Greenock Motor Services Leyland Tiger TS7 with Burlingham body in service on Bute. New in 1937 it was withdrawn in 1957. *SJB collection*

In 1965 all of Rothesay's double-deckers were Leyland Titans. These included this 1948 PD1 with 1952 ECW body. The bus had been new to Greenock Motor Services with Strachans bodywork. *SJB*

In 1969 this was the cover of the summer timetable for services on Bute. The illustration is a splendid anachronism and shows a 1949 AEC Regent III with Duple body - a combination never operated by Western. Buses of this type were operated by Scottish Omnibuses but had all been withdrawn by 1966 - three years before the appearance of this timetable.

The Bute Open Top Experience in 1999, being operated by a Bristol VRT. The company has also operated open-top Daimler Fleetlines and Leyland Titans. *SJB*

In the late 1990s most services on Bute were operated by Leyland Nationals. This 1979 bus, repowered with a Gardner engine, had been acquired with the A1 business in 1995 and was one of relatively few ex-A1 buses to survive any length of time with Western. It had been new to Crosville Motor Services and spent some time with Blackpool Transport before joining the A1 fleet. *SJB*

Arran

LONG A POPULAR destination for all sorts of tourists - from climbers to sight-seers - Arran's bus services were provided by a surprisingly large number of small family businesses. In 1958 there were seven companies running 40 buses, most of which were Bedfords and none of which seated more than 30 people. Many services were timed to link with steamer sailings, and there was a healthy business in providing round-the-island tours in conjunction with the arrival of steamers from the mainland.

The 1960s saw the arrival of bigger vehicles - secondhand half-cabs in the main - and the start of a process of gradual consolidation. As in Bute, the introduction of car ferries and the rise in car ownership had a significant impact on the island's bus services. By 1973 there was just one significant operator on the island - the Arran Transport & Trading Co, running around a dozen buses. Arran Transport had been created in 1967 with the merger of Lennox of Whiting Bay and Lennox Motors of Brodick. The only other surviving operator, Bannatyne of Blackwaterfoot, was purchased by Arran Transport in 1973.

The availability of the government's new bus grant saw the island's bus fleet transformed in the 1970s, with new Bedford Y-series buses and coaches replacing older vehicles. In 1984 the Strathclyde PTE experimented with an unusual Dodge GO8 truck chassis fitted with a demountable 20-seat bus body built by Marshall. The idea - which harked back to the very earliest days of bus operation - was that the vehicle could have its bus body removed so that it could also operate as a truck, therefore increasing its utilisation and spreading its operating costs over the transport of both passengers and goods. It was not a success.

When much of the island's bus network was put out to tender by the Strathclyde Passenger Transport Executive in 1992 Western, at that time management-owned, put in a successful bid and established a base at Brodick with a fleet of 12 buses. Arran Transport retaliated by setting up an operation on Bute at Western's expense.

The Western operation on Arran has continued under Stagecoach ownership, and in 1994 Western purchased the Arran Transport company's bus interests. Unlike Bute, Arran has no history of double-deck bus operation and what is thought to be the first on the island arrived in 1995 with the introduction by Western of an open-top tour.

In 2000 Western had 16 vehicles on Arran, a mixture of full-size buses and coaches and Mercedes-Benz minibuses.

This is Brodick in 1965, with a selection of vehicles collecting passengers from the car ferry from Ardrossan. The vehicles belong to four operators - Bannatyne, Weir, Ribbeck and Lennox - and are of Albion, Commer and AEC manufacture. *SJB*

This AEC Regal III in the Lennox fleet had bodywork built in Prestwick by Scottish Aviation, one of the pioneers in the use of aluminium for bus bodywork. It joined the Lennox fleet from A1 Service. Note the ex-military Bedford truck delivering soft drinks. *SJB*

In 1985 Arran Coaches was the main operator of the island's bus services. Its fleet included this Bedford YNT with bodywork by Wright of Ballymena. Wright would grow to become a major supplier of bus bodies to British fleets, but was still a relatively small builder when this body was supplied to Arran Coaches in 1983. *SJB*

The Strathclyde Passenger Transport Executive briefly experimented with this dual-purpose Dodge on Arran. The bus section of the body could be removed - note the vertical rubber seal where the front and rear sections of the body join. In its place a van body could be fitted for delivery work. The experiment was not a success, and the Dodge normally ran as a bus. *SJB*

In 1995 Western introduced an open-top tour on Arran using this one-time Midland Scottish Daimler Fleetline with Alexander body. The bus dated from 1970 and had been re-registered during a period of ownership with Clydeside Scottish. *Murdoch Currie*

AA MOTOR SERVICES was formed as a limited company in 1931. It was a co-operative of seven operators with 16 buses who began working together in the previous year, as a breakaway from the A1 business. It operated between Ayr and Ardrossan, and soon added services from Ayr to Annbank and Irvine to Stewarton. Local services were established in Irvine, partly through the acquisition of North Ayrshire Coaches in the early 1950s, and these were expanded as Irvine developed.

The number of members who constituted the co-operative fell as the years passed by. By 1960 there were three - Dodds, Tumilty and Young. Tumilty withdrew in 1972 and Young in 1992, so when Western took over in 1997 AA was owned by Dodds of Troon - the Dodds family having been involved in AA right from the start.

A wide variety of new and used buses have been operated by AA over the years. Single-deck Albions were the dominant type in the 1930s, but after the war the characteristic types were Guy Arabs and Leyland Titans, giving way in the 1960s to Fleetlines and Atlanteans. The Guys, favoured by Dodds in particular,

Seddon buses were never commonplace. AA operated this 1949 example which was one of a pair with bodywork by Aburnson. It is seen in the company's Ayr bus station.
S N J White

Foden built just over 50 double-deckers in the late 1940s and early 1950s. A few were bought by Scottish fleets, including AA which operated this 1948 PVD6 with angular bodywork by Welsh Metal Industries.
A B Cross

were often the subject of extensive rebuilding and rebodying to maximise their operating lives. At the other extreme from the rebuilding of old Guys, AA was one of the few independent operators to buy new Leyland National integrals - regarded at the time as a complex high-tech bus. These were owned by Young, a confirmed Leyland user over many years.

AA's buses were green and cream and the fleet strength has been remarkably stable over the last four decades at around 40 vehicles. AA Buses was adopted as a trading name in the 1980s.

AA ran both double- and single-deck Daimler Fleetlines. These included this former Tayside bus. The chassis dated from 1970, and had been rebodied by Marshall in 1980, at which point the bus was re-registered. It joined the AA fleet in 1984 and is seen at Irvine Cross in 1985. *SJB*

AA was one of the first small operators to buy Leyland Nationals. Initially it bought new examples - starting in 1972 - but from the mid-1980s started buying used Nationals. This 1977 bus was bought from West Midlands Travel in 1990. *SJB*

Under Stagecoach ownership new buses were introduced to the AA fleet in 1997. These were Dennis Dart SLFs with Alexander ALX200 bodies and were the first buses in the area to be accessible to baby buggies thanks to their step-free entrances. *SJB*

A1 WAS THE biggest and best-known of the Ayrshire co-operatives. Formed as the Ayrshire Bus Owners Association in 1926 with around a dozen members, it quickly grew and established itself as the main operator in the Kilmarnock - Irvine - Ardrossan corridor. This was a period of rapid change, but by 1931 when a new company, Ayrshire Bus Owners (A1 Service) Ltd, had been formed, there were 22 members, each running two buses.

Membership changed over the years, as did the rules controlling the types of vehicles which could be operated. New buses were the norm in the 1930s and the late 1940s, but the 1950s saw secondhand double-deckers joining the fleet - in particular redundant London Transport RTs and RTLs. At the start of the 1960s the members agreed that no buses over five years old should be bought. This rule was soon relaxed - but the advent of new bus grant saw a massive intake of new double-deckers in the 1970s, many of which were still in operation when Stagecoach bought the business in 1995.

When London Transport started selling relatively modern RT-type AEC Regents in the late 1950s, A1 was an enthusiastic buyer and the fleet was quickly updated with ex-London buses. This smart example is seen passing Parkhouse Garage as it enters the A1 bus station in Ardrossan. This is a 1965 view, before the time when petrol stations were required to display prices in large figures visible from the road. *SJB*

Single-deckers were relatively uncommon in A1 Service operation. This is a 1947 AEC Regal with bodywork by Croft of Glasgow, photographed in the mid-1950s in Ardrossan. Note the Ministry of Labour and National Service office in the background. *S N J White*

A1's buses were blue and cream with maroon relief, but applied in a variety of styles which reflected the individuality of the owners. This individuality could also be seen in the types of vehicles bought.

While the company's core operation remained in central Ayrshire (and was boosted by the growth of Irvine New Town), in the early 1980s it took advantage of coach deregulation to introduce express services to Glasgow, generally operating at peak periods only and using coaches.

In 1940 A1 ran 40 vehicles, all single-deckers. By 1965 this had grown to 62, all of which were double-deckers, and in 1990 the total stood at 80. When Stagecoach took over A1 had ten members from whom it acquired 67 buses, most of them double-deckers.

Among the older buses which Stagecoach acquired with the A1 business was this 1976 Alexander-bodied Atlantean, still in A1's colours but with Stagecoach fleetnames. It is seen on the seafront at Ardrossan. *SJB*

When coach services were deregulated in 1980, A1 introduced limited stop services linking Ayrshire towns with Glasgow. These used a temporary coach station in Glasgow on the site now occupied by the Concert Hall. On the left is a Leyland Tiger with Duple Dominant body bound for Ardrossan, and on the right a Volvo B58 with Wadham Stringer Vanguard body which is loading for Dundonald. *SJB*

Very few ex-A1 buses received Stagecoach colours. One which did was this unusual Volvo Citybus with East Lancs body. Built as a Volvo demonstrator in 1983, it was purchased by A1 in 1985. *SJB*

Coaching contrasts

Handsome Burlingham coachwork was fitted to this Leyland Tiger PS1, one of 24 delivered in 1948-49. *SJB collection*

From 1952 to 1955 Western operated this unique coach, an Albion KP71NW with Scottish Aviation body. It was Albion's first underfloor-engined model but any plans to develop it were ended after Albion was taken over by Leyland in 1951. This coach was in fact an Albion demonstrator, and was returned to its manufacturer. *Garry Ward collection*

The Albion Aberdonian featured a Leyland engine, and three joined the Western fleet in 1957. The glass louvres above the side windows were an unusual feature to find on this style of Alexander body and were designed to reduce draughts when the sliding windows were opened. The three Aberdonians were transferred to sister Scottish Bus Group company Alexander (Northern) in 1965. *Harry Hay*

Coach interiors were sumptuous in the 1950s. This was an Alexander-bodied Guy Arab UF. *Garry Ward collection*

The first imported chassis in the modern Western fleet were eight Volvo B58s delivered in 1975. These had 42-seat Alexander M-type bodies. One passes Central Station in Glasgow, in black-and-white London livery. *Robert Grieves collection*

Stagecoach is the only British operator of articulated coaches. All are Volvo B10Ms with bodywork by either Plaxton on Belgian builder Jonckheere. This is a 72-seat Jonckheere Modulo. *Murdoch Currie*

ONE OF WESTERN'S predecessors, Midland Bus Services, started running an express service from Glasgow to London in 1928. It was taken over by the newly-formed Western SMT company in 1932. For such a long service - 400 miles end to end - Western provided its customers with high standards of comfort. London coaches had generously-spaced seats, overnight passengers had a tartan travelling rug, and from 1951- responding to the challenge of a new service introduced by Northern Roadways of Glasgow - an on-board toilet compartment was fitted, although there were still refreshment stops en route.

Prior to the building of motorways, the route headed south by the A74, then across the A66 to Scotch Corner and south to London via the A1. The A1 passed through a number of towns on its way south - such as Doncaster, Newark and Grantham - although as by-passes

were opened the opportunity was taken to use them to reduce end-to-end journey times.

Because of the high mileages covered - often over 100,000 miles a year - the coaches used on the London service tended to have relatively short front-line lives. The average life was six years although after as little as three years some coaches on the London run would be transferred to other less arduous coaching duties or, on occasion, sold to other operators.

The coaches used were often Leylands. There were Leyland Tigers in the 1930s, followed by stop-gap rebodied Leyland Lions when the service resumed in 1946 after being suspended during World War II. Leyland lost its supremacy on the London run in the 1950s when Western ran AEC Regal IVs and Guy Arabs, but a new Leyland model, the Leopard, was introduced to the London service in 1960.

Diesel engines gained quick acceptance in the early 1930s but were still a novelty when Midland tried this diesel-powered AEC Regal on the Glasgow to London service in 1932. It is seen leaving the new Victoria Coach Station in London. The body was by Wycombe. The Midland Regals are generally acknowledged as being the country's first diesel-engined express coaches. *Gary Ward collection*

Legislation allowing longer coaches saw the arrival of 36ft-long Leopards in 1963, with 38 seats compared to just 30 in the previous models. These had striking Alexander Y-type bodies, with the Western name carried on an illuminated panel on the side.

The Leopards were followed by Bristol REs. The first were outwardly similar to the Leopards, but in 1969 a new look arrived for the London service with the delivery of the first of an even

For over half a century one of the most prestigious aspects of Western's operations was the Glasgow to London service. From 1951 to 1955 it was operated by 14 Alexander-bodied AEC Regal IVs which had 30 generously-spaced seats, and a toilet compartment in the rear nearside corner. These coaches had been built for Scottish Omnibuses - hence their Edinburgh registration numbers - but were diverted to Western to counter competition from new operator Northern Roadways. The location is Dundas Street Bus Station in Glasgow. These were Western's last new AECs. *SJB collection*

bigger coach, the 12m-long Bristol RE with 42-seat Alexander M-type body. These were inspired by America's Greyhound coaches and had double-glazing - a UK first. The mid-1970s saw a switch to Volvos, initially with Alexander bodywork but, from 1981 with Duple Dominant III bodies which had trapezoidal windows to match the general appearance of the M-type.

Major road improvements brought time savings for London passengers. In 1965 the end-to-end trip time was scheduled at 13 hours 50 minutes, but by 1971 this had been cut to 11 hours for the traditional route, or to just 9 hours for a new direct route using the M6 and M1 motorways and running non-stop apart from picking up or setting down in Carlisle and stopping for a refreshment break at Charnock Richard services, on the M6 just south of Preston.

Up until 1976 the London coaches were in Western's unusual black and white livery, but in that year the Scottish Bus Group introduced a new identity for its London services, using a blue and white livery with the fleetname "Scottish" alongside a stylised saltire. Following coach

deregulation in 1980 SBG had a rethink on all of its coaching activities and adopted Scottish Citylink as the brand name for express services, including from 1985 those operated by Western to London which now included routes from Wemyss Bay and Gourock via Greenock, Ayr, Paisley and Glasgow, and from Stranraer. The Stranraer service provided connections with ferry sailings to Larne and onward to Belfast or Londonderry.

The mid-1980s saw a range of new types being used including a variety of twin-deck coaches with a small passenger compartment seating around 10 people behind the rear axle. These coaches, seating around 60, were Van Hool Astrons and Volvo B10Ms with Plaxton Paramount 4000 and Berkhof

Emperor bodywork. Three Duple 425 Integrals joined the fleet in 1985.

Full-size double-deckers were used too, initially MCW Metroliners, then in 1986 three new Plaxton Paramount 4000s on Scania chassis, later joined by two used examples. They provided Scottish Citylink's equivalent of the National Express Rapide service - branded Cordon Blue - with the second driver dispensing hot drinks and sandwiches.

Rationalisation of express coach services by National Express and Scottish Citylink brought an end to Western's involvement in operation from Glasgow to London in the early 1990s, although the company still operates on the Stranraer to London service using two Volvo coaches in Eurolines livery.

At the southern end of the route, London's Victoria Coach Station, a 1954 Guy Arab LUF with Alexander body arrives to pick up passengers for the 400-mile trip north. There were ten of these coaches, and they were used on the London service until 1960. *SJB collection*

In 1960 Western bought 20 Leyland Leopards for the London run. These were the company's first new Leyland coaches since the Tigers of 1949 and they were the mainstay of the operation until 1966. Like previous London coaches they were 30-seaters with a rear toilet compartment. *SJB*

In 1966 there was a significant improvement to the London fleet, with the delivery of 21 Bristol RELH6Gs. These were longer - 36ft instead of 30ft - and could thus seat 38 people. They had Alexander Y-type bodies which had big fixed side windows and forced-air ventilation. The rear-mounted engine of the Bristol RE helped minimise interior noise. *SJB*

A new generation of even bigger coaches arrived in 1969, with delivery of the first 12m-long Bristol REMH6Gs with Alexander M-type bodies featuring double-glazing and an auxiliary oil-fired heating system. The styling of the 42-seat body was clearly influenced by US practice. When new the M-types were in Western's traditional black-and-white colours. By the time of this 1978 view, the corporate blue and white Scottish livery was being used for London coaches. *SJB*

Western in Dumfries

The Paisley registration of this Guy Arab II in Dumfries points to its origins in the Youngs' fleet. New in 1945, it has a Northern Counties body. It was withdrawn in 1962. *SJB collection*

A trio of Bristols in Dumfries in the early 1960s. Nearest the camera are two Lodekkas. The single-decker is an Alexander-bodied MW, a combination unique to Western. *John Burnett*

The predominantly black livery used by Western at the time the company was bought by Stagecoach could produce a rather sombre appearance, as illustrated by this Alexander-bodied Seddon in Dumfries. An identical bus, on the left, in Stagecoach colours looks much brighter. *SJB*

Caledonian

THE MAJOR OPERATOR in the far south-west of Scotland for just over two decades was the Caledonian Omnibus Co. It was formed by the BET group in 1927 to unite five small businesses running 46 buses between them. Its head office was in Dumfries.

The company expanded by acquisition at the start of the 1930s, notable take-overs including in 1931 Farrer & Faulder of Carlisle (13 buses) and South of Scotland Motor Co (21 buses), followed in 1932 by Harper of Peebles (28 buses). New buses in the 1930s were mainly Dennises, all single-decked. Where small buses were needed, Caledonian bought Thornycrofts.

Double-deckers were first operated in 1938, with the purchase of four second-hand eight-year-old

Leyland Titan TD1s. More soon followed, and by 1941 there were 28 TD1s (plus two AEC Regents) in operation. The outbreak of war had seen the establishment of a number of military bases in the area, along with new factories geared up to supporting the war effort. This created new business for Caledonian. New buses during the war were primarily Bedford OWBs, 16 of which were delivered in 1942-43.

The BET and Tilling groups had combined their bus interests in

The Caledonian fleet included a number of prewar Dennis Lancets, and two of these were fitted with new ECW bodies in 1948. They were operated by Western until 1957. Alongside stands a 1947 AEC Regent II with Northern Counties body. *A B Cross*

Tilling and British Automobile Traction in 1928, an alliance which lasted until 1942 when they split. Caledonian then became part of the Tilling group. When the war ended Caledonian continued to receive standard Tilling group buses - ECW-bodied Bristols; the first of

Dennis Lancets were favoured by Caledonian in the 1930s. This 1935 bus has a Weymann 32-seat body. *Charles F Klapper*

these had been delivered in 1938. Ten L5Gs with rear-entrance bodies were delivered in 1946-47, followed by the company's only new double-deckers, four Bristol Ks in 1948-49. In fact only two of the Ks were delivered to Caledonian. The second pair were loaned to London Transport, and by the time they arrived in Scotland in early 1950 Caledonian had been acquired by Western SMT.

When Caledonian was taken over by Western it had 138 vehicles ranging from 20-year-old Titans to its brand-new Bristol Ks. These survived until 1963, at which time they were the last ex-Caledonian buses in Western service.

Only four postwar Bristol Ks with ECW bodies were bought new by a Scottish operator: Caledonian. Two were K6Bs with Bristol engines in 1948, followed by a pair of Gardner-powered K6Gs in 1949. This is the second of the K6Gs and was the last bus bought by Caledonian. It is still in Caledonian colours but devoid of fleetnames and fleetnumbers in this summer 1950 view. These were the last ex-Caledonian buses to see service with Western. They were withdrawn in 1963. *A B Cross*

The only modern single-deckers in the Caledonian fleet when it was acquired by Western were 10 Bristol L5Gs with rear-entrance 35-seat ECW bodies. New in 1946-47, they were withdrawn by Western in 1960. One is seen in Carlisle bus station, ready to leave for Dumfries. *S E Letts*

The radiator might say Leyland - but this is in fact a 1936 Albion Venturer, which Western acquired with the Caledonian business. Caledonian had bought this bus - and three others - from Glasgow Corporation in 1944 and then had all four fitted with new bodywork by Croft of Glasgow in 1947. They were operated by Western until 1957. *A B Cross*

Dumfries independents

Carruthers of New Abbey provided a service to Dumfries and among the more unusual buses in its fleet was this Foden PVD6, bought new in 1947. It had a Scottish Commercial body. Note the period Post Office Morris van on the right. *SJB collection*

Gibson's operated from Moffat to Dumfries. This 1943 Guy Arab II with Weymann body joined the fleet in 1954 and was owned until 1960. It had been new to Liverpool Corporation. *SJB collection*

The operations of Clarks' of Dumfries were taken over by Western in 1965. This Bury Corporation Leyland Titan PD1 with Roe body was bought by Clarks' in 1959 and operated until 1964. It is seen arriving in Dumfries. A smart Vauxhall Cresta with two-tone paint scheme and metal sun visor stands at the kerb. *A B Cross*

Western in Ayr

Poor-quality timber framing in the nine Strachans bodies supplied to Western on Leyland Titan PD1 chassis in 1949 led to the bodies being scrapped after just three years, with replacement bodies being supplied by ECW. This rare photo of a Strachans-bodied PD1 was taken in Ayr in the summer of 1950 before there were any indications that all might not be well with the structure. *A B Cross*

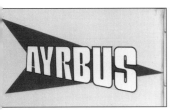

Small numbers of Daimler double-deckers were purchased by Western in the late 1940s and early 1950s. This 1948 CVA6 has an AEC engine, pre-selector gearbox, and lowbridge Northern Counties body. It is seen in Ayr bus station in the late 1950s. *SJB collection*

The Ayrbus name was used for a short time in the 1980s, as shown on this Seddon Pennine VII with 53-seat Alexander Y-type body. *SJB*

Rebodied

Two consecutively-registered Guys in Ayr show the difference a new body can make. Eleven Arab IIs were delivered in 1945. In 1953 two of were fitted with new lowbridge Alexander bodies, and one of these is seen in the bus station. The other bus, at Burns Monument has its original Northern Counties body. The new bodies did not extend the lives of the vehicles involved. All were withdrawn in the early 1960s.
SJB collection

The combination of Albion chassis and ECW body was unusual. Western had four such buses. They were ex-Youngs' Venturers which were rebodied by ECW in 1953. The chassis dated from 1938. This one is seen in Dumfries. *Roy Marshall*

In 1946 Western took delivery of 40 AEC Regal single-deckers with Burlingham bus bodies. In 1954-55 12 of these were given new ECW/Bristol double-deck bodies. One is seen in Largs, with Castlesons distinctive building just visible in the background. These buses were withdrawn in 1963. *SJB collection*

In 1994 Western had two redundant London coaches rebodied as 51-seat buses by East Lancs. The chassis dated from 1980 and 1981 and had originally carried Duple bodies. *Billy Nicol*

New in 1936 with a Leyland body (see page 8) this Titan TD4 was fitted with this new Northern Counties body in 1949 and operated until 1960. It is loading for Neilston in Clyde Street, Glasgow. *SJB collection*

In 1948 Western bought 12 Sheffield Corporation Leyland Titan TD4s, dating from 1935-37, which they had rebodied with new 33-seat Burlingham coach bodies before putting them into service. To most passengers they would have appeared to be new coaches. *A B Cross*

Scottish Citylink

To combat competition from new express coach operators, all of the Scottish Bus Group's express services were marketed as Scottish Citylink from the autumn of 1983. Among the more unusual and least luxurious coaches to carry the two-tone blue and yellow Citylink colours were a few 1979 Seddon Pennine VIIs with Alexander T-type bodies in the Western fleet. These operated on the service from Glasgow to Tarbert. One passes through Ardrishaig in 1985. *SJB*

The Alexander T-type was dramatically restyled to produce the stylish TC (C for Coach) which used the same body structure, but with new square-cornered tinted glazing, and restyled front and rear. In 1987 Western took six 55-seat TCs on Dennis Dorchester chassis, four of which wore Citylink colours. *SJB*

To succeed the M-type on the London service , Western bought a new style of Duple body, the Dominant IV, which copied the M-type's main styling feature - small trapezoidal side windows - albeit without the panache of the original. This Dominant IV, on a Volvo B10M chassis, was one of 12 delivered in 1981. It is seen in 1985 in Scottish Citylink colours. *SJB*

From 1948 to 1995 Western used a system of two-letter prefixes to its fleet numbers. The first letter showed the garage to which the bus was allocated, while the second indicated the vehicle make, generally using the first letter of the chassis manufacturer for a single-deck and the last letter for a double-deck. The codes used were:

First letter (garage, including related sub-depots)

A	Ayr	M	Newton Mearns (Thornliebank from 1968)	S	Stranraer (from 1977, previously D)
C	Cumnock	N	Ardrossan	T	Ardrossan (from 1995 for the A1 fleet, but not carried on the vehicles)
D	Dumfries	N	Arran (from 1994)		
E	Carlisle (1977 to 1987)	O	Cowal (from 1994, but not carried on the vehicles)		
G	Greenock Inchinnan Johnstone	P	Paisley (from 1977, previously J)	Y	Islay (1979 to 1985)
K	Kilmarnock	R	Rothesay		
L	London service coaches (from 1986)				

Second letter (vehicle type)

A	AEC sd (until 1964)	D	Dennis dd (from 1983)	N	Albion dd (until 1979)
A	Ailsa dd (from 1978)	D	Dodge minibus (from 1987)	N	Dennis sd (from 1983)
A	Scania coach (from 1986)	E	Bedford sd (from 1970)	R	Daimler dd
A	Leyland Atlantean (from 1991)	G	Guy sd	S	Dennis sd (until 1957)
B	Bedford sd (until 1954)	H	Hestair Duple 425	S	Seddon sd (from 1975)
B	Bristol dd (also ex-Caledonian Bristol sd until 1960)	I	Albion sd	T	Bristol sd (from 1957)
		L	Leyland sd	T	Talbot minibus (from 1989)
C	AEC dd	M	Maudslay sd	V	Volvo (sd and dd)
D	Leyland dd (until 1980)	M	MCW coach	Y	Guy dd
		M	MAN-powered Van Hool (1986 only)	Z	Mercedes-Benz minibus

Thus, for example, DL999 was a Dumfries-based Leyland single-decker.

In addition, from 1965 to 1977 each vehicle carried a code alongside the fleet number showing the year in which it was built. This comprised the letter A for the 1950s and B for the 1960s (and later C for the 1970s), followed by a number for the year - thus B2 indicated 1962.

Leyland Leopards with Alexander Y-type bodies were used by Western for a wide range of operations. Two 1968 examples are seen here at the Barony pit, near Ayr waiting to take workers home. *Garry Ward collection*

The West Promenade at Rothesay, with a 1920s canvas-roofed single-decker
heading towards the pier head. The tram lines have been lifted but the granite setts remain and the people at the bottom o
the picture are waiting alongside a stop on which the flag reads "Car Stopping Place". The card, by Valentine's, was poste
in 1943 and has printed on the reverse: "This is a time for everyone to stand together, and hold firm!" - The Prime Minister

The Colintraive Ferry with a coach gingerly making its way
down the ramp was an eye-catching subject for the photographer in this late 1970s shot of a Y-type
Seddon with its passengers waiting patiently behind. The postcard was by Dennis Productions.